Journeys of sobriety by five recovering alcoholics.
Each one of them sharing their experience,
Strength and hope, that someone reading these short stories of their lives, will get a powerful message in their daily living.

YOU ARE NO LONGER
ALONE
Author Peter   L

Anonymity is the spiritual foundation of Alcoholics Anonymous. In that tradition, the author and persons sharing have decided to withhold their last names on this book which chronicles their gradual spiritual transformation

From the Author

Hello everyone

My name is Peter L
And I am an alcoholic

Do you have a drink problem ?
Do you know of someone who has ?
Do you live with a problem drinker?

In this book, five recovering/recovered alcoholics share their lives in the hope that a powerful message can be passed to the still suffering alcoholic.

If you love an alcoholic, but, are distraught with that person's behavior, then you might just find out something of real benefit to you.

There are many different help organizations that are there just for that reason. Some of them will be listed at the rear pages with general help contact details.

Every one of us that have recovered and sharing, are members of Alcoholics Anonymous.

Many of the people sharing have had dealings with Rehab centers. Some of us were introduced to AA meetings while detoxing.

I can only talk for myself, AA was the only thing that helped me achieve sobriety. However! There have been some great starting blocks in detox units for some of us too.

For those of you who know nothing about Alcoholics Anonymous, I would ask of you to look up the information and maybe if you have a computer, do a search for the Big Book of Alcoholics Anonymous. As

members, when we share, we sometimes use the term. (BB). I think most of you will be fascinated when you- - discover how AA was started back in the nineteen thirties, and how much the fellowship has grown since then.
Even more surprising, the fact that the first two members of AA were a New York stock broker, and a Doctor.

Here are some of the signs about alcoholism.
Common signs of alcoholism include:
- "Being unable to control alcohol consumption
- Craving alcohol when you're not drinking
- Putting alcohol above personal responsibilities
- Feeling the need to keep drinking more
- Spending a substantial amount of money on alcohol
- Behaving differently after drinking".

This list could go on and on.

Alcohol abuse can lead to short- and long-term health problems.
Some of us sharing have had this problem but have gone on to recover physically.

Several short-term effects of alcohol abuse may produce:
- "Slow reaction time
- Poor reflexes
- Reduce brain activity
- Lowered inhibitions
- Blurry vision
- Difficulty breathing

• Restlessness "

Here are some of the long-term health conditions caused by alcohol:
- "Brain defects.
- Liver disease
- Diabetes complications
- Heart problems
- Increased risk of cancer
- Vision damage
- Bone loss "

Once again, we could add many more.

" *When we feel we have lost hope, we may find inspiration in the words and deeds of others.*" Author Quote Unknown.

Life can be tough! It can swallow you up, chew you to pieces then spit you out like a garbage disposal unit. Sometimes! Without help, it becomes over-powering

December 23, 2018

When I started to put this book together, my youngest son was taken into hospital in South east London.
I live in Sweden, so emergency measures were taken for me to acquire an emergency passport from British Embassy in Stockholm.
For the first time in over five years, I managed to see, hug, and tell him "I loved him." Face to face.

Spending many hours at his bedside, we spoke a lot about how he ended up where he was.

"Dad! I have a drink problem!" He said to me teary eyed. Of course, I had known of this for many years, but I was powerless over his situation. Many times, I asked him, then waited for his replies.

What was coming back to me was denial.

There is an old saying.

"You can lead a horse to water, but you can't make it drink."

This was the case for my son.

Most people when having a problem, will only except the solution when they truly one-hundred percent admit and believe to the said problem.

My son told me laying critically ill, that he had stopped drinking four weeks before and was surprised that he had been on a life support machine, oblivious to what had happened. He thought because he had stopped drinking, he was fine!

At that point! The doctors had only given him a one-percent chance of survival.

With us living thousands of miles apart, he knew I had to return to Sweden.

My Swedish wife of five years was starting her fourth treatment of chemo that same day, for her third time cancer. I was torn between two situations that I had no control over. The emergency passport was valid just a couple of days, so had no option but to return home.

Before I left London, my son began to improve. He was starting to eat some food, sometimes managing to keep it down and not throwing up. Each day after, I kept in contact with the hospital and my son.

His chances were getting better as each day passed.

There was a relief in my heart. Over the next two weeks,

he was moved to a medical ward from Critical care unit. Many sighs of relief each day and thanking the God of my understanding.

I heard from many friends from around the world, each one sending prayers of hope for everything that was happening. Everything was out with my control, and I sat back and handed each day over to This beautiful Higher Power.

On Friday December 21st, 2018, I had a phone call from my son's half-sister. She was breaking her heart as she told me of the new situation in his recovery.

"He is back in critical care and on a life support machine for the second time." She said. Two hours later she called again.

"The doctors say the next forty-eight hours are crucial to determine if he would survive."

On December 22nd, 2018. At 7.54 pm. My youngest son Wayne passed away.

Alcoholism is a destroyer of worlds. Peoples worlds.
So why am I writing this less than 24 hours since his passing?
I searched on line on how to deal with grief in sobriety. Many items lead me to doing things that I liked to do. One of them was writing.

My Higher power, God as I understand him gave me a gift. The gift of writing. Considering that I was slow and found myself in the bottom of most classes at school, I didn't think I could achieve this idea.

March 2015, I found myself starting to write my first book and by the end of that year, I had a fifty-seven-thousand-word book. No one was more amazed than me. Not bad for an ex-drunk.

In the time since then, I have published five books. The

sixth has been put on the back burner which is seventy-five percent completed.

"Walking in the sunlight of the spirit."

This book is more important for me to write than any other. Maybe you can see why?

I don't mind if this book doesn't sell many copies. I am not taking any royalties for this book, and I am donating my copyright for this book to charity. The most important thing is this.

If ONE person who reads the short stories here can change their life for the better, then I have achieved what needed to happen. If more than one, then wow!

If you have a drink problem!
There is hope!
Look hard enough, and you will find the right solution for you!
My son doesn't have that choice now. You do!

I am grateful today for my life and sobriety.
I thank God as I understand him for guiding two drunks together back in the 1930s who started a fellowship that has grown by the millions in many countries worldwide. WOW! What a gift.

<u>Self will run riot</u>

PETER L

Hi everyone.
I am an alcoholic and my name is Peter.

First, let me say how grateful I am for my life and sobriety today!
So, many of you might be asking yourself how I know I am

an alcoholic? How do I qualify for that title? Let me share as best I can on my life and journey to where I am today.

Going back in my mind as far as I can, I can remember when I was about three years old. Even at that early age I was afraid. Not understanding fear then, but with hindsight that's what it was. A frightened little boy who felt lost when not around family or friends.

My Mother, God love her did her best to feed and clothe us and worked hard to do so. Mom was a nurse some of the time, she spent long hours caring for others.

I remember her wonderful smiles as she looked down from what was to me a great height. My brother Graham was two years older than me, and we have a saying in the UK." Butter wouldn't melt in his mouth!" In other words. He was the favorite. Did I know what jealousy meant at three or four years old? Nope! But that was what I was full of.

I had many kids around me where we lived, some were true friends. Playmates!

What I noticed around them was their mothers and fathers. Then it dawned on me. Where was my father? I didn't have one!

To this day I don't remember who told me about my father, but what I do remember is being told that I was seven months old when he was killed in a plane crash while returning to the UK in 1957.

Again, with hindsight, I can see why my mother was very emotional most of the time. I was sad when she was. I held her legs sometimes when tears would run down her cheeks.

Looking back. I had many beautiful childhood memories. Some of those memories were of my grandparents. They only lived a ten minuet walk away.

I loved them dearly.

Grandad Reg! He was like the missing father I didn't have, I worshipped the ground he walked on. That's where I felt safe. I felt wanted needed and loved.

He helped buy me school clothes and shoes many times, so that Mom didn't have that hidden financial burden.

My world as I lived in it, came crashing down one day, when Graham and I were told that Mom was getting married, and we were going to have a new Dad.

For whatever reason, and to this day, I have no idea why we never met him until the day of their wedding in our Devonshire town in England.

Affordability meant that the reception was held in our home. From our bedroom window, Graham and I could see the old church in the far distance. We also had German measles or chicken pox! Not sure which.

We were told to stay in the bedroom and not come out until someone came for us.

Not long afterwards, the bedroom door opened and in came my favorite uncle, Moms brother. I can still remember his deep soft-spoken voice as he came over to us and lifted both of us in his arms.

"Hi my handsome boys!" He had an aura of kindness about him, and I thought that I would have loved him to be my father. Again, jealousy showed its ugly head at such a young age. This time jealous of my cousins.

So, he took us downstairs and into the wedding reception. I remember looking around the room. I saw many family members, and friends of the family. Then I saw this stranger, very tall and bright red face.

Mom picked me up and walked over to this man.

"This is your new father Peter!" she said smiling. A cold shiver went through me as I looked at this face. Fear engulfed my whole body. There was something about him I didn't like.

In fact, it was everything about him I didn't like.
I jumped out of Moms arms and ran over to my grandfather.
I began to feel safer straight away.
I am sharing these situations as I know many of us have had
similar experiences.
The main point is that fear will dictate to us a lot of how we
react later in life, and how we deal with it.
In the safe environment with people we care about, and who
care and really love us. We don't feel alone.
That all was to change as I grew older.
My life from that point changed dramatically.
I always felt uncomfortable when I was at home. I was very
cautious when my stepfather was there. He had one of those
voices that you could hear for hundreds of meters if he was
shouting for you. Even if he spoke quieter, he still sounded
like a drill sergeant in the army.
As I said, my safe-haven was at my grandparents. I spent a
lot of time as I was growing up in that love environment.
There was one day my step-father came down the garden
path, he was so angry.
He told my grand-father that, "He spends that much time
down here, he can stay for good." Guess who felt like the
happiest young boy around?
 Hence to say Mom was getting a hard time from him, I
returned a couple days later.
It was in those first couple of years that I started to see him
come home from the bars, mainly on a Friday evening, but
sometimes on other days at holiday times. His excuse was he
was playing in the local domino leagues. Mom used to call it
an excuse, anyway!
From all those early years I know he never lifted me up,
hugged me, or ever said. "I love you son, or Peter."
He had a daughter and a son within those years. My half-

sister and half-brother.

Graham and I were left out of a lot of activities in their times growing up.

My stepfather often said things like. "We can't take Graham and Peter with us today, they can stay at their grandfathers house." Suited me perfectly.

Then came the day I came home from school and heard horrendous shouting and hearing mom scream.

That was the first time I saw a drunken man beating up on a woman. I was terrified. I had that vision for a long time. Like a video recorder, I would play the scene over and over until I cried for the mom that was treated like a punch bag. I vowed that I would never hit a woman in my life when I grew up. Thank God. Even for all the crazy garbage I put people through later in my life. I kept that vow picturing my mother firmly in my head.

So, I saw many times, problems after problems. Most of them around were caused by alcohol.

Most people around me who had sporadic drinking sessions were fine, happy, and seemed to enjoy their social drinking. Then there was the odd person who drank, then some arguments would come out in conversations. Each person then trying to get their point across! Some of them threatened violence towards each other. When I saw that, it scared the life out of me. I remember asking myself, "What is happening with these kind people?" I was so confused as to how someone nice could turn so quickly violent in manner. It was about that time I saw a movie on TV. It was "Doctor Jekyll and Mr. Hyde."

The story as most of us knows, is how the doctor invented a potion that when he drank it turned him into something completely different. He became fearless, he became quite clever, and became cunning and powerful to gain peoples

trust. Basically, he was manipulating, deceitful, and becoming evil. The result was that he didn't have to take the potion, he was changing automatically without it.
Now where have I heard that before? "Oh yes!" Every time I look back at my drinking life, that's where.
So, at a very young age, I was introduced to some people who had an abnormal reaction to alcohol. One moment, they were great, they were kind, many spoke quietly, and when drinking took place, they changed for the worse.

I remember also being at my grandparent's house, when the day came, I was introduced to alcohol. My first ever alcoholic drink. To me it was something that only adults could partake in, but, as it was a cold snowy day in winter, Gran was giving her neighbor some cherry brandy to warm her up. Right or wrong, Gran poured a very small amount into a brandy glass, then said. "This will warm the cockles of your heart!" Old English saying.
I had a glowing smile on my face as I drank it down quicker than I drank soda-pop.
WOW! What a feeling. The warm glow hit my stomach, I loved the taste of every drop. It was so good, I asked Gran for more. Ha-ha. "No!" She said laughing. I didn't like that answer, so I got moody and went to my bedroom there and sulked.
I felt though that something in me had changed. Just a very small amount had made me feel taller, not so frightened, and fell like I was super man!
Many times when Gran or Grandad got the magic potion out, I was like a puppy dog waiting to be fed.
The memory of that first taste put many an expecting smile upon my face.

That was the start of my introduction to alcohol. I only had a small nip of the elixir

In the next years leading up to leaving school at sixteen, I didn't do very well at school. I hated being there most of the time. I used to skip out of classes using lies to do so. For example. Saying I had dental work to be done, or going to asthmatic therapy, which I did have at times, but lied when I didn't.

I found through a lot of my teen-age years, I was becoming very nervous, very afraid most of the time. I was having bad nightmares which I couldn't explain. I was beginning to withdraw into myself. I would get on a bus, hoping that there were not many people on it.

My step father still scared the pants off me and withdrew even more into myself. He was now saying I was a useless person, I was an idiot, and you will never get any-where in life. I felt like a piece of garbage. I wasn't doing well at school, but hardly one person said anything nice about me. Never encouraged me.

Through the school, I joined the surf lifesaving club on the Southwest coast near our school. I got qualified as a lifeguard, and then was on patrol at a young age of fourteen. That year, to that point in time, the club had never been called into action to help another person in danger in the sea. Within that weekend, my brother, a girl at school called Susan, and myself managed to save five persons from rough seas. The reason I talk about this is this.

We were famous. Everyone was talking about these three kids who saved five people in two days. And guess what? I loved the attention. I became boastful to my school friends. I thought it was good to tell others that I had done good deeds. To be honest. I was conceited. My head grew bigger and bigger, some kids at school began to avoid me. I was bullied a lot at times, and eventually as I went through the year grades, I became the bully. Picking on smaller kids in their first year. I am not proud of that. Later, in life, I managed to make amends to some I had harmed. If I ever come across any people, no matter where, I Tell them I am truly sorry for the harm I did. Each situation that arises in my life concerning that, I evaluate each case separately, as I do not want to harm them again by doing so. But the point is I am willing to do so. You see looking back. I was wrong and hurtful many times. Long before my drinking took off big time. I found out that Me! Peter had many defects of character. I was self-seeking even then. The great I AM!

I thought I knew everything, but I knew nothing.

After leaving school I had the chance to go in the merchant navy. Family and friends were happy for me to get the chance to travel the world. My first ship was an oil tanker, one of the biggest around at the time.

Just a few days into the voyage, one of the older deck hands said he was having drinks after our shift that day. Would I like to come? Ha-ha. Can a duck swim?

Here I was. Sixteen years old, getting paid good money for travelling around the world, and enjoying duty free booze that I didn't need to buy. So, the party began with about five of us.

I remember small pieces of that night, but most of it was a total blackout. I squinted my eyes to see myself laying half in and half out of the safety rails at the ships starboard side. How the heck did I get here? Was my first thought.

Next was me coming around and being dragged down to my cabin.

When the early shift officer woke me the next morning. Well! God did I feel ill. I have never felt that way in my life before, to that point in time.

My head spun like a tornado, I felt physically sick and proceeded to throw up. I was sweating profusely. Trying to focus on what had happened the night before, I remembered the start of the drinking session, I remember the warm glow as the rum hit my stomach, then the feeling I was like a giant, and invincible like I felt the time my gran had given me the cherry brandy.

I remember laughing and joking with the guys, I remember singing a bit, and I couldn't sing! I felt like I just belonged in this world, and I didn't have any fear what's so ever. Wow! The elixir of life. So, I thought.

The officer told me I looked ill. He wasn't kidding. He said he would get the chief steward who was also our medic on board. Opening my eyes again, he was standing over my bed saying, "Wow! You look grey and ghastly. Best place for you is in bed today! I will get the chef to make you some hot bread and soup later."

Maybe twenty minuets passed, then the chief came in again. "Right young man! I heard you were drinking last night! Innocently, I replied.

"Yes sir!" Well, he started to laugh, and I didn't think it was a laughing matter. How dare he laugh at me being sick.

"What you have is commonly known as a hangover! Now get your butt out of bed and get to work!"

I will not swear in this book, but you can probably guess what I said? The second word was "OFF"

He certainly wasn't pleased at my reply, and looking back, he had every right to be dis-pleased.

The outcome of that first drunk was that I refused to work for three days. I was ill for the seventy-two hours.

So, trouble came right at the beginning of my drinking. I swore off booze, vowing never to touch the stuff again.

But as time went on, I forgot how bad I was feeling in that first drunk. I am not sure how long it was until my next drinking session, however, I wanted to drink, I wanted that feeling of fitting in again, to also take my fears away but hoping I wouldn't get as bad as I did the first time.

I was drunk in anticipation of drinking.

There were many times I went out drinking, tried to drink sociably, sometimes I managed to get home, where ever home was at the time. There were times that I didn't remember anything about the night before, but people were so quick to tell me what I had done. I would laugh it off and say things like." That was crazy last night Huh?" I had no clue what I had done, who I might have hurt.

When I look back at those crazy times, I didn't know I had an illness, I didn't know that when I took that first drink, something happened in me that doesn't happen in average temperate drinkers. Many hangovers later, many cuts and bruises, I noticed that I was shaking, fears were entering my life again but on a bigger scale.

In 1985, I ended up in Scotland where my father was from. To be in the land where I came from was exciting.

I found a lot of relations on dads' side and I started to settle down to a new way of life.

I was one of those guys that people were glad to know me, then, as time went by, they were keeping well away from me. Either I lied to them, cheated them, or for whatever self-seeking reason, they quite rightly walked away.

I was ashamed at times when I was confronted with the truth of my actions in my drinking bouts. But then somewhere in that day, I got hold of the booze and as I drank it, I started to change again. Maybe I wasn't that bad yesterday, maybe they exaggerated my actions. Maybe they were just full of bull-crap.

I homed in on a wonderful woman who had a pub. OMG! I was in heaven, so I thought.

Here I was, thinking I was in love with this beautiful lady, and I had the chance to drink as much as I wanted.

So, I thought, wow! When in Scotland, drink like the Scots do! So, I did. But here's the cruncher. Most human beings don't drink like I do! I believe that maybe ninety-five percent who drink do not have a problem with it. Yes, there are some very heavy drinkers, but they get on with their life. Then you have the people like me who when drinks, cannot control drinking, or stop. The craving in me was incredible.

I could not drink with safety, and I had no idea what would happen when I lifted that first drink, whatever it was. Rum, Vodka, Whiskey, Beer. I chased the alcohol and whatever gave me that buzz and took away my fears, it didn't matter.

I was now in a drinking environment that helped justify my drinking. I started to notice that I was shaking a lot and knew if I took some measures of alcohol, the shakes would stop, for a while.

It wasn't long before trouble started up again in my drinking. My mood swings were progressing, I started to get panicky and full of fear again. Sometimes I knew where trouble would start in the pub. I needed to be tanked up to deal with it.

When I was half tanked, I could jump into three or more people who were fighting. I remember one night, we had seventeen start a bar fight. I was in the middle of them trying to break it up. I had two under one arm in head locks, and my other around the throat of one guy. I was feeling invincible again.

Time has a way of catching up with you if you drank like I did. And it did.

There came a time when fighting broke out unexpectedly, you

then could find me being a frightened coward in the office, afraid to come out.

Liz my fiancé decided that the best thing for me was being put in charge of the off-sales shop at the side of the pub. Keeping me out of harm's way, and a lot safer for some of the customers as I was resenting their every movement.

It was at that time when a lot of sneaky drinking came about.

Being by myself in a small room wasn't appealing, until, I realized that the room was full of quarter, half, and full bottles of booze. Putting me in charge of an off sales shop was like putting a wolf in charge of a sheep pen. Many times, I poured some coke from a can, then picked up some booze from a shelf and into the coke-can.

Occasionally, staff from the pub, or Liz would come in with a large glass of alcohol to keep me company.

Strange words to say booze was keeping me company, but it was my friend, it was my anti-depressant, it was my master, and this guy didn't know it.

I could list two books with all the crazy things that happened in my life, but I will get to what happened that changed my life.

It was getting to the stage now that I was so afraid to go out the house, when I did, I drove the car everywhere, and many times driving drunk. Liz and I were arguing nearly all the time. Mainly, it was to do with her bringing home booze from the pub. I played on my situation and told her I was just feeling ill all the time, it would be better for me to drink in the house. An odd time she brought some staff home to join us in social behavior. For me, it was all about what drink they would bring.

I volunteered to be the drink pourer in the kitchen, and you can guess now that everyone had small amounts, but me? I had ninety-nine percent of the glass filled with whatever poison I was drinking.

I remember friends of ours sitting down in the living room. I like always poured them small amounts, and me my usual large glass of the magic elixir.

I was feeling pleased with myself that I had got one over on them, again. Only as I sat down, I knocked my glass over. To this day, I don't know what stopped me from getting down on the glass coffee table and licking it up like a dog.

I was so angry, so bitter and twisted inside. There was no more left. I stormed out of the house sulking as usual and drove drunk around the beach area of the town.

That night, I was arrested for DUI. I knew when the cops started following me in an un-marked police car that I was caught.

I raised my hands up to the cops and told them I was totally drunk and will come quietly

Crazy thing was that the cops said I was the best drunk driver they have dealt with. Not a good thing to have cops tell you, "you were a good drunk driver."

Later that night, when I returned home, Liz had gone back to the pub and got more alcohol. Now I could calm down a little. Drank a full glass down in seconds, and then partial blackout.

I smoked at that time also and tried to focus my drunk eyes on a road that I was staring at below me about twenty meters. I was fumbling for a cigarette and finally managed to light it.

I was sitting on a road bridge at the edge with my feet dangling off it.

I was crying my eyes out, big strong macho type guy that I thought I was.

I thought through my drunkenness and decided I was

ending it after I had finished my last few cigarettes

Of course, when you sit on a road bridge dangling legs over the side. You attract attention. It wasn't very long before police sirens raced to the bridge I was sitting on. They blocked the road below and both sides of the bridge.

I was aware they were there, but I didn't care. Why should I? Drunk, wasting police time when they could be out catching real criminals. Crazy insane thinking and all the time wondering who might come to my funeral when I was gone. Lighting another cigarette, I slurred my words to the cops as they asked if they could get anyone to help me. There was only one person that I could think of, that was my practice Doctor. He always listened to me when I went to him.

"Please don't jump Peter!" I heard one of the cops say.

I was confused as to how they knew my name was Peter. Guess somewhere along those drunken conversations with them, I mentioned who I was.

What I forgot was, that my second cousin on my fathers' side was a cop. He had been called a while ago to the pub one day when I assaulted a customer. So, most police officers knew who I was.

Probably about thirty minuets passed when I squinted my eyes along the bridge road, and walking towards me was my Doctor.

I burst into tears again and asked him "If he could help me?" I wanted to end it all, but, as time was marching on, I was returning to the horrendous fear that was building up in me again. I was scared that I would jump but didn't know how to live! I am so grateful I didn't have the courage to go through with that.

The police took me to the main hospital and I saw the duty psychiatrist.

 He only asked one question. "Do you still want to kill

yourself?" Of course, I didn't, so he said, "Well then! You are free to go!"

I was now starting to sober up a little and staggered out of the hospital even more confused.

Waking up laying in bed, Liz had already gone to get the pub ready, and I went back to sleep until I heard the front door bell.

Trying to focus my bloodshot eyes, standing on the porch were a man and a woman smartly dressed and smiling.

They introduced themselves to me as Alex C and Christine D. "We hear you might have a drink problem Peter? Liz got in touch with Christine and we thought you might like help?" I was still a people pleaser and didn't want to offend them by saying "No!"

So, inviting them in, they started to tell me they were members of alcoholics anonymous and they were sober a few years.

The funny thing was that I used to serve Christine alcohol a while back and then one day she disappeared, and I never saw her again, until that day.

They said that I was probably helping them more than them helping me. That at the time didn't make sense to me, it would be a long time until I knew what they meant by that.

Christine took the lead and went to make us all coffee as I was incapable of controlling my shakes.

The result of that first encounter was them inviting me to an AA meeting later that day. They would pick me up and did so early evening.

In the car, I couldn't understand how two smartly dressed people with a very expensive car could call themselves alcoholics. I guess I always had visions of an alcoholic as the guy sleeping on the streets and on park benches. But as I said before, I thought I knew everything about everything, but I knew nothing about nothing.

The building where the meeting was held was belonging to the town council, it looked like a mansion.

I couldn't believe my eyes when I went inside. Christine and Alex started to introduce me to all the men and women standing and sitting. "This is Peter, and it's his first meeting!"

Well, I had nearly every person come up and told me I was welcome, and If I had a drink problem, I was in the right place. Some kept saying. "We love you, Keep coming back!"

OH, I thought I was in with some real weirdos.

I remember my first resentment towards an AA member when the guy doing tea and coffee handed me just half a cup! But one member watched my expression on my face and said to me. "Its half full because we don't want you burning yourself as your hands are shaking quite a bit." To me, it was half empty! Ha-Ha! That was me. Always looking at the negative side of things rather than positive.

They ushered me to the front of the hall and sat me down. I guess there were around seventy people there that night,

In a lot of U, K, Scottish meetings the format of the meetings are someone chairs the meeting, and someone sits next to them at the top table and shares their experience strength and hope, then they share around the room, time permitting.

I sat on my hands most of the meeting, trying not to let people know I was shaking because of booze.

My mind was still fuzzy from the night before, and one part of me wanted to run like hell from the room, and the fearful side told me to sit my butt down and not draw attention to myself.

I had been looking around that room that first night, I saw so much laughter and smiling. I had a problem believing they were alcoholic.

Even bigger problem was that I didn't believe I was alcoholic. I knew at times I drank too much, but I wasn't that bad! I am laughing at myself right now thinking that. And that's ok. I understand today why I felt that way.

So, when I heard the speaker. Then people sharing around the room, I thought it was a competition to say who had done the most damage in their drinking. WRONG!

I was looking at all the differences, not similarities.

That was my introduction to AA, and I went to many meetings, didn't lift the first drink, and started to say at meetings. "My name is Peter, and I am an alcoholic."

I didn't believe that. I said it because all the people in the meetings said it.

I did start to feel a little better when in the rooms, but I was feeling that AA wasn't for me. I stuck around the meetings for six weeks, dry! I was secretly planning my next drink, and when one night I got back from a meeting, Liz asked me how I was.

I told her "I'm not as bad as those people, I can handle a few drinks!" She agreed with me. I know today why she agreed with me.

You see, she was my drinking buddy, and for six weeks, she lost that. I found that out much later.

The next day, I went back to work, and many customers in the bar said they were glad to see me back, and some offered me a drink. That sounded like a good idea, especially as I was planning drinking anyway.

The first, second, and third day, I watched carefully how much I was consuming. If it was only a few, I was going to be ok.

I can smile at that. Because you guessed it. The fourth day I ended up drunk, and the fifth, and the sixth. Within less than a week, I was drinking even more than I did before I stopped six weeks previously.

The drinking became more secretive, hiding what ever I could from people around me. If I was in town and I had money I would walk into many different bars, so it looked like I was just having one or two. But by the time I got to the third or fourth bar, some managers asked me to leave. To me that was ok. There were many others to choose from.

I was so sick, and I didn't know it.

I was getting in trouble with Liz and the staff. Once again being put in charge of the off sales shop.

A repeat of arguments with Liz, trying to chat up female customers, and ended up fighting with some customers who were mostly sat enjoying their drinks, until I upset them in one way or another.

I had one of those what I call next day attitudes. The next day I would be saying sorry to so many people, it was pathetic. Then, somewhere in that day I would lift that first drink. The roller coaster journey started again.

Do you remember what I said in the beginning of my story? How doctor Jekyll changed even though sometimes he didn't take the poison? Well yes! It was happening to me.

I could see it every time I looked in the mirror. I hated what I was looking at.

There was one day a regular customer came into the bar, he was chatting up Liz and trying his luck. The problem was he was part of the local Scottish mafia. He was the big shot. He had spent many a time in jails and decided he would get educated. He earned himself a PHD while serving a couple years for violence and firearms offenses. There was one day he had a fight with another gangster in the lounge bar. The result of that was his six shooters fell out on the floor and I ran to pick it up and put it in the safe in the office while the fight was still going on.

In my mind when I held the gun, I felt powerful, wouldn't it be cool to have my own gun? Crazy thinking huh? The worst was yet to come.

I was becoming so angry and resentful at him taking Liz's attention away from me, I was full of paranoid jealousy. Every day, I would visualize myself killing him. Yes! I was planning his murder.

The crazy situation was getting out of control in my mind, it was so twisted with hate and evil intent. I hated thinking evil thoughts, but as more drink passed my lips, I felt justified in my thinking actions, and he deserved to die. I am glad once again my cowardice overtook me.

In an eighteen-month period since my first AA meeting, I was consuming about two forty ouncers of booze every day, and I still didn't think I was drinking too much.

Again, I withdrew to drinking in the house. Afraid to venture outside most of the time. I plucked up enough courage one day to see my doctor.

Same doctor who had come to the bridge to help me eighteen months earlier. He asked me what I thought he could do to help me. I knew I needed help now, but I didn't want to go to AA, as that hadn't worked for me.

He told me he could admit me to a psychiatric hospital, and they might be able to get to the root of my problems. He was honest with me, he told me he thought there wasn't much hope for me unless I stopped drinking. I agreed to be committed and he arranged for me to go in the next day.

Liz was nervous when I told her the news, then she agreed that maybe I did need to stop drinking.

On the twenty third of August 1989, I lay in bed crying my eyes out yet again, only this time the pain was so great in my mind and shaking like a rock and roll singer on stage, I cried out to the universe. "Whoever you are, whatever you are, if you are there. Please help me. I can't take this anymore." After being admitted the next day, I sat by myself. The fear was so great, the other patients came over to me and I began conversations with some.

Deep down I was wondering who the real crazies were, which one of them was going to kill me first? Those first hours in that day saw a lot of paranoia.

I told you I was most of the time a people pleaser in my life, always trying to please others. Well, on the twenty-fourth of August 1989. I became the people pleaser one last time.

The nursing staff came over to me about seven that evening. "Peter! This is Ann S, she is from alcoholics anonymous. We think you might like to go to an aa meeting with her, and she will take you and bring you back."

I forced a smile then found myself saying "Yes! Of course!" The meeting she took me to, happened to be the same meeting place I had gone to eighteen months previously. All I could think of was getting back to the crazy ward and safety.

The warm welcomes I had been given the first time were still there. People telling me they were "Glad to see me," They shook my hand, again half cups of coffee, but this time, there was something different in the room.

A member came up to me and said. "The only requirement for membership is a desire to stop drinking!" That was it! That was the miracle words I needed to hear at that moment in time.

A miracle did happen for me at that meeting.

You see, the night before, I pleaded and screamed at the universe, "If you are there, whatever you are, please help me." The first step in AA is. "We admitted we were powerless over alcohol, and that our lives had become unmanageable. I honestly admitted and accepted that first step in its entirety. My existence was a wreck. Booze had beaten me into surrender. All these years in my drinking, it was the lack of power. Booze was more powerful than me and kicked my butt time and time again.

I looked around the room again, and this time, I saw the laughter and smiles still there, but I was aware why they were happy. This was the higher power that they spoke of working with them. When at least two recovering alcoholics come together for the purpose of sobriety, A power greater than booze sits with them.

Step two is. Came to believe that a power greater than ourselves could restore us to sanity. I was a total raving lunatic and nutty as a fruit cake. Booze had pounded me for years and beat me.

At that moment, a surge of energy engulfed me, and I knew that somehow, some way, If I did what they suggested I do, things beyond my wildest dreams would happen.

The third step in Alcoholics anonymous.

Made a decision to turn our will and our lives over to the care of God as we understood him.

I handed my will and life over right there and then to a God I wasn't sure of, but knew one day at a time, I would.

Here's one of the great bits for me.

23rd August 1989.... I hit my rock bottom. I asked for help, honestly.

24th August 1989.... I surrendered and accepted Alcohol had beaten me.

24th August 1989.... I started believing in a higher power/ God.

24th August 1989.... I made the decision to hand my will and life over to this higher power/God as I did or didn't understand him to be.

I asked for help. He sent me the fellowship of Alcoholics
Anonymous and true friends. Sober people who had been
exactly where I had been and no where else to go. I was
heading for total insanity or death.
The miracle for me was having the obsession removed at that
meeting.
I sighed with relief as a small smile came to my wrecked
grey white face.
From that day, I attended many meetings one day at a time.
I wanted to know more about the recovery program and
started reading the Big Book of Alcoholics Anonymous.
Just under my first ninety days sober, I realized that I
needed to get out of the pub work, and this meant looking for
another job.
I didn't want to be around a drinking environment now and
proceeded to look in the Scottish national press for work.

Riding the train about then, I was heading to Edinburgh for
an interview for a real-estate position in the Canary Islands.
Most of the journey was me smiling a lot. Something was
telling me I had this job, but I didn't know how I knew this.
Every day sober was the beginning of something new,
something powerful in my life was guiding me to some of
my wildest dreams.
Sitting opposite this tall American man, he was well dressed,
spoke calmly and quietly. He asked me to tell him about me,
and I proceeded to tell him.
Only ten minuets into the interview he stopped me and said.
"Peter! You don't need to go any further. You have the job!"
Wow! I was so excited. As I said, I knew I had the job when on
the train. The best was still to come.
He was telling me of a beautiful Island that was sixty miles
long by forty-miles wide with a dormant volcano in the

mountains. He presented a great picture. He also described the fantastic night life there. Then he mentioned that there was a lot of cheap alcohol and you can afford to get drunk there a lot, if you wish.

Just a few seconds, a fear returned in my life. I was beginning to think carefully before I spoke. I thought that I would tell him I don't drink.

What surprised me when I told him was, he replied straight away. "Are you on any program for not drinking?" He asked.

I began a slight panic as I wondered whether to tell him. Again, something powerful was telling me to be honest and tell him.

"Well sir! I don't drink today, and for me, its not an option. I am a member of alcoholics anonymous!"

He got up from his desk, came around to the other side and asked me to stand up. Now I was thinking he was going to throw me out the room. Ha-Ha!

He grabbed me and hugged me and said. "Hi Peter! My first name is David, and I am an alcoholic too, sober one day at a time seven years.

OMG! Anyone could have knocked me over with a feather at that moment. WOW!

On the train earlier, I had been thinking if they had AA meetings on the island, and hope there were other aa members to help guide me.

David asked me to help him with the remainder of the candidates as a few more places were available.

At the close that day, he took me to the hotel restaurant and bought me dinner.

"Have you got a sponsor to help you Peter? He asked. I had temporary sponsors and members phone numbers, but no one long term.

"Ok! I'm your sponsor now! Its Our higher powers will for us to help each other!"

I liked that idea a lot. That day, I stopped believing in coincidences and believed that God was now in the driving seat, and I loved where he was taking me.

When I returned home to Liz that day, I asked God for the strength to tell her what I needed to say. I was to meet David in Glasgow in two days, then do other business in London, and fly to Canary Islands which David arranged flights for me.

Liz was pleading with me to not go, and she wanted me back drinking. I told her that my drinking days were over today, and I was not wanting to drink.

Remember I said earlier that I knew why Liz had said many things back in my drinking days? Well yes! It was because we were drinking partners and we justified each other's drinking.

I walked away from that lady, and the bar. A sense of true freedom came over me. I was happy this great higher power was in my life and showing me a life that I was just about to embark on. One day at a time.

So, my dear friends and you dear reader.

What am I like today?

On the 24th August 1989. I came back to a wonderful fellowship of ex drunks who guided me with our higher powers. God of our own understanding. The members I had met around the world were caring, and they taught me well in the recovery program. The 12 steps of Alcoholics Anonymous.

I have had two heart attacks. Ulcers. Diabetes. Exploding

blood vessels in my stomach.

Continuous heart problems. But you know what?

Older age does not come by itself Ha-ha!

Today! January 2019. I am 29 years 5 months sober One day at a time.

Thanks to GOD! The 12-step recovery program, and the fellowship of people who guided me. Members of AA

I have a life today. Not an existence.

I know who Peter is today. I'm still finding out beautiful things in my sobriety. I am not cured of this disease of alcoholism. I have a daily reprieve from a nightmare life that by lifting one drink could return. So just for today. I choose not to drink. Let God run my day as he sees fit. Attend meetings. And pass on to others that was freely passed on to me.

My spiritual journey is just started. Yes! Each day is a new start. I have sober eyes today that are wide open, and I remain openminded to each day.

When I hand my will and my life over each day to a loving Higher Power. More things are revealed to me.

So, is there life after booze?

If you are truly alcoholic, and you desperately need help. Yes! I came. I came to. I came to believe.

Today! I am walking in the sunlight of the spirit

I dedicate my share to my dear son Wayne. Rest peacefully son. We will meet again.

THANK YOU FOR READING MY SHARE

I STARTED DRINKING IN THE 8TH GRADE

Hi Everyone, I am a sober alcoholic and member of Alcoholics Anonymous.

I appreciate very much this opportunity to share "my story." Much more important than what got me here is what has happened to me since I've been here. I do not think any alcoholic comes to AA for fun, or to attend a social outing, but they come because they are desperate to find freedom from a life of death and destruction caused by their dependence on alcohol. AA has a solution.

I say that's most important because I have recovered from a seemingly hopeless state of mind and body and if you are sitting here sick and tired of being sick and tired... I want you to know that if it happened for me, it can happen for you too, through this program.

I started drinking in the 8th grade, Boones Farm Strawberry Hill...

I wanted to be popular, to fit in and I remember it made me so sick. But I was hooked! I loved it from that very first time! It 'relaxed' me, it made me 'funny', it gave me 'courage.'

I had no courage when I got to AA... I had been beaten down by King Alcohol almost to the grave. I would get up every day and swear I would not drink and by noon would be well on my way to oblivion.

I tried every way in the world to stop drinking on my own to no avail. I didn't have the courage to stop drinking for even one day because I was afraid if I did, it would be expected all the time of me. I came through these doors full of despair, afraid and alone. I had annihilated everything and everyone good in my life.

I am not going to get into all the "uglies" much- we have all been There or we wouldn't be here.

I can just tell you that because of my alcoholism, I have seen abuse, broken homes, lost jobs, a dui, all the way to Walmart's fitting room as a bathroom- alcoholism is not pretty. Our Big Book (Alcoholics Anonymous) says that, "An alcoholic in his cups is an unlovely creature." Real alcoholics will understand what that means.

I thought I was the most easy-going person in the world when I came to AA...all I needed to be happy was my booze. I could not see how my need for alcohol was hurting those I love. I didn't realize that one of the reasons I drank is because I was eaten up with, consumed with victimhood.

32

I mean, in the end, drinking was never a pleasant experience, but rather an act of anger, self-pity, remorse, guilt, etc. I was always drinking At something or Over someone

My husband would tell me he was concerned for me and that I needed to stop drinking...In a rage I would say, "The one thing I enjoy in life and you want to take it away!" UGH- talk about EGO! Can you imagine, a wonderful husband, four beautiful boys, and the One thing I wanted was my alcohol?! Well, yes, I am sure some of you imagine this quite well.

I always had a reason to drink.... It did not matter to me if my best friend had died or was getting married, if my husband cheated or bought me roses, if the sun came Up or went Down...what I learned in AA years later is that I drank because there had come a time in my disease that I had crossed a certain line and could not find my way back on my own...nor through any other human aid.

My first year in AA I constantly heard "Don't drink and go to meetings," and "90 meetings in 90 days." Now I am not saying those are bad suggestions, they are good suggestions...the problem for me was that neither suggestion could keep me sober. I stopped at the liquor store on my way home from every meeting and would start early enough the next day to sleep it off before going back, or so I thought.

I struggled badly my first year here, only managing to put together 112 days without alcohol.

I came went to Online AA and saw people share and laugh. I went to face to face meetings, and people were hugging and smiling - All without alcohol and I wanted that freedom.

So, I did what was suggested... I read the Big Book every day, I went to meetings every day, I had sponsors and unfortunately, I could not stay sober. (I didn't know then what I know now...I was missing the Steps of the AA program).

Looking back now I can see that much of my failure in A.A. was due to the lack of The message being carried here in my area. But, also, it was due to my own selfishness. I felt like I showed up, now A.A. should be doing something for me and it wasn't working. I didn't realize that A.A. only works if you work it. It is a program of action that is a "design for living," if applied to one's life.

When I finally hit my bottom and decided to ask for help with my problem, the first lesson I learned was the severity of my disease. I went to this man in sheer desperation and asked him to show me what he was doing that I was not...why the steps were working in his life, and not mine.

I am forever grateful that he was willing to share with me what was shared with him. In order to fully concede that I was an alcoholic, I needed to know just what that meant. My sponsor explained that alcoholism is a three-fold disease.

It centers in the mind and that is why even after long periods of time without alcohol, the obsession to drink is still there. Then, after we give into the drink, as we often do, the physical allergy sets in and our bodies tell us we have to have MORE. Alcoholism I learned, is also a spiritual malady and that when the malady is overcome, the mind and body straighten out as well. So, I realized for the first time what I was up against. I did not have a "bad habit," or a lack of moral values, but a very real disease that would kill me if not treated.

My sponsor led me through the steps as they are outlined in the Big Book and showed me how to Apply them to my life...not just to read them, but to live them.

In step one, I admitted from my gut that I am an alcoholic, committing to the fact that I can Never drink again safely. In step two, I came to believe that my God could restore me to sanity. In step three I turned my life and my will over to God...meaning I would seek His will rather than my own. In step four I made a list of my resentments and took my responsibility for my part in them....

I shared those resentments with my sponsor in the eyes of God and agreed to right any wrongs as best I could. I became willing to let God remove my shortcomings in step six and humbly asked Him to in step 7.

THIS is how I straightened out spiritually...it happened naturally through the steps and as our Big Book promises, my obsession to drink was removed. I don't suspect I will ever want to drink again so long as I maintain my spiritual fitness on a daily basis, which is what the AA Program calls for the alcoholic to do.

Today, I work to do that by living in steps 10-12 every day. The only requirement for membership is the desire to stop drinking for the Fellowship of A.A. The A.A. program, however, suggests certain things I must do if I expect to live happily in this world without alcohol.

Step 10 tells me that I must continue to take personal inventory and promptly admit any new wrongs along the way. Broken down that means when selfishness, dishonesty, fear, resentment crop up, I must 1. pray immediately for God to remove them, 2. talk about it with another person immediately, 3. make amends quickly if I have harmed anyone, and 4. resolutely help another alcoholic. With step 10, I continue to grow in effectiveness and understanding of my relationship with God.

Step 11 is one of prayer and meditation. The BB tells us that if we want to stay sober, we must carry the vision of God's will in every part of our lives. My nightly inventory is a review of my day... I ask God's forgiveness for my shortcomings and his guidance to correct any wrongs for the day. In my morning inventory, I ask God to direct my thinking throughout the day, that it be free from self -will- Thy will not mine be done.

Step 12 tells me that I must carry This message to other alcoholics. Sharing the message plays a vital role in my own recovery...and...the BB says that I can help where no one else can. I think it is truly amazing that I might even help to save a life today when there was a time I could not even help myself.

I love this program and I am grateful for the life it has given me today. If I could tell you the most important thing I am trying to convey out of this share, it would be that if you are a suffering alcoholic, there IS a solution for you to be found in AA.

The solution is IN the steps and you truly do NOT have to drink anymore. Get to many meetings, make good use of the Fellowship, they have been where you are, find yourself a sponsor, and work the steps. Continue to apply the steps to All your life and you can obtain and maintain sobriety! AA is a wonderful way of life and I am grateful to be living it. I am 15 years sober which flabbergasts me, but I always remember, it all started with one step, and has continued 'one day at a time.'

Freedom in the Sunlight of the Spirit

I was mired in the prison of alcoholism. I was sick physically, mentally, and spiritually.
I lived in that inner darkness.

The steps of desperation 1 through 3:
I realized I needed help.
Yes, my drinking was way beyond normal. My life was totally unmanageable.
Alcohol wasn't working anymore; insanity reigned.

I needed something beyond myself to get me to the right place; I could not do it myself, obviously, looking at where I had brought myself with the assistance of alcohol.

So, my HP interrupted my drinking in August 2015. I do not know how or why.
I don't understand it. I do not need to understand.
It happened and I am grateful it did. I surrendered.

I was told I needed to change; have a shift in attitude and perception in order to have a better life. I had the willingness to accept that I was an alcoholic

The steps of perspiration 4 through 9:
I was told I needed to work for it; ACTION!! This is where the blood sweat, and tears came into play. The real work begins.
The thorough moral inventory; not easy looking at myself and deep inside myself; seeing it in black and white; real me?

Then the willingness to move forward.
Admitting my wrongs to the God of my understanding was the easy part; then came torturous difficult admission about myself to myself.

But what took the cake was telling all of this "me stuff" to another human being.
Telling EVERYTHING! Rigorous HONESTY!

Asking my HP to remove all my defects and shortcomings?
What will be left of me? It's all I knew.

Listing all people, I had harmed; quite an undertaking.
THEN willing to make amends! Whew!
Direct amends; finding courage; what would be the outcomes.

Hard work? You bet! Physical, emotional and spiritual sweat.

The best thing for me. It all leads me to this point in my sobriety.
Reflection, prayer, taking personal inventory, making amends, service and more are now part of my 24 hours.

Steps 10-12 the steps of INSPIRATION.

Inspired by what I have learned since 8/7/15 in the AA fellowship,
I am evolving daily into the real me, sometimes quickly sometimes slowly;
Applying my tools and strategies to live the life and be the man I was meant to be.

Opening myself up to the grace of my HP.
Passing on what I have learned to others in and out of the fellowship in my daily affairs

Renewing and re-dedicating myself each morning for the coming 24 hours; living in TODAY, feet firmly planted Live in the moment dealing with what's put in my path with the guidance of my HP.

Well, every day isn't all sunshine, lollipops and rainbows, mind you, but it sure beats the insanity of my life before I was given the gifts of willingness and acceptance; allowing my HP to work within me, the gift of the fellowship of Alcoholics Anonymous, discovering more and more about this alcoholic called Daniel.

It's for a lifetime, a way of life, living and maintaining a meaningful sober life.
I am truly grateful for this new and exciting journey.

The burden of my past is being left by the wayside bit by bit; a lightening of that heavy load that held me down. Yet, there is still work to make things even lighter.

Being a small part of the fellowship of AA is in itself a tremendous privilege.
Where else is there an organization that carries on year after year and maintains Unity with the purpose of keeping it alive by helping one another with humility, compassion, love, and tolerance.

I cannot take this journey of freedom alone I attend meetings, I meditate and pray. I work through the steps with my sponsor. I sponsor others, I am active in the fellowship, and pass along to other alcoholics what I was freely given.

I carry it from the fellowship to my life outside as best I can. I need to reach out to others in need AND reach out to others if I am in need.

Every morning I wake up with untreated alcoholism. I know what to do now.
I surrender every morning. Every day is my first day of sobriety. With willingness and gratitude, I give my will and life over to that power greater than myself. I use the tools and strategies

that I learned in the program and the fellowship to turn my life around. Every day I open myself to the light and grace of my HP remembering I only have today.

Not every day is perfect sometimes I try and take my will back, but there is progress.

I was once told alcoholism is the only prison with the key inside. I remind myself every morning to use that key given to me by that power greater than myself.

Giving of myself and being of service to others in recovery are essential for feeding my own recovery. I give and get back. I am twice blessed.

I have been given a gift: this new freedom in the light. A new way of living life on life's terms.

I am grateful to my HP for guiding me here. I only have today and embrace that new freedom.

If I keep my thinking and words positive and follow up with healthy actions, life goes right.

This is my Plan A. There is no Plan B for me. The miracle, the solution is happening.

It is summed up for me in the Promises:

Feelings of freedom and happiness.
Gaining a deeper perspective.
Renewed purpose or direction in life.
Acceptance of self and others.
Selflessness.
Hope and faith.

Less fear and/or financial worry.
Redemption from past actions.

Today I walk in the Sunlight of the Spirit.

Alcoholics Anonymous places no demands on me.
Once I entered, I am free to leave.
If I leave, I am free to reenter.
If I stay, I remain sober.

Peace be your journey in the Sunlight of the Spirit.

Daniel G.

Experience strength and hope

A good set of words.

My journey into and out of Alcoholism started at birth I believe. My
dad had the genes and I got em.

That being said there's more to this story then I got the genes I got
sick and I got well. I will try and tell my story or at least a part of it.

I can remember a very nice memory of drinking which gave me a
very slippery slide into a world I wouldn't be able to get out of for 10
years.

In 1972 I was 18 and my buddy and I would down a bottle each of
colt 45 and go into town and dance up a storm. During this time, I
also for the first time had great success auditioning for a play.   It
was the first time I had the courage… better said the splashing wild
freedom to be myself and act up a storm in front of others. And
seriously it was all because I had the booze behind me. Inside me. I
was loaded and it worked.

Now to be honest this made sense.
If something works for a young man
who for all his life
was incapable of being himself
cause of his learning differences he got squelched repeatedly…
And now because of alcohol he can easily get a super power of
sorts
 It makes him capable
He can do what he's all ways dreamed of doing in public.
He can shout or not, cry or laugh freely or not, he has the ability to
act up a storm
with no inhibitions.
This was a big plus.

I didn't return to be in the play I did so well auditioning for because I didn't have the ability to come back and do the great acting I had done while under the influence. Alcohol wasn't available to 18-year old's easily.
I was able to get it easy later and I did regularly.

I drank and I drank, and I drank for 10 years.
I knew my life was going nowhere.
A lady I used to drink with had gotten sober through AA.
She had the audacity to ask me to join her at an AA meeting.
I said sure I would maybe the next week.
She said how about tonight? I'll pick you up.
(In side my head I heard the words …"do it now or you might not get a second chance to have a life").
So, I went to an AA meeting. And I stuck with the program for 13 years. It worked. I loved being sober.

Buttttttt

I only did the steps up to step 5.
I stopped going to my regular weekly meeting around year 10.

Year 13 when I was out of the country
I met some people that made their own beer and whiskey.
I thought to myself
"I can always stop! I did it once I can do it again."

Part of this incredible 'intelligent thinking I was having' ha-ha.
Intelligent my ass. But part of the thinking when like this

"I'm a wild child. A one of a kind. I'm not like 'them' (other alcoholics).
I run a different machine of thinking. I can do what I like.
Cause I am controlled by a higher source than what those others are controlled by.

A God that allows me to act independently and learn my own way!
Then here comes the big one;
"Those people don't know what I know!"
What the heck I knew that you didn't I can't really say….
 because it really was hog wash.
But it was something like a cosmic mind of the Aquarius generation.
We are better cause we know Free Love and all.

I felt like I had fallen from God's grace.
I slipped into a deeper and more hideous darkness than I had ever known.
23 years after I started drinking again, I decided to join AA in the way that I hadn't before.
Lock Stock and barrel.
All the way!
No holds barred.
I was in.
I went on my knees,
got a sponsor,
did the steps,
go to meetings, and
work the program the way I see fit.
It's a good thing.
I'm not better or worse than all my wonderful friends and associates in AA. I'm just a plain old drunk who needs help. I can't drink alcohol and I can't do it on my own.
Alcoholics Anonymous is my way for the rest of my life one day at a time.
 I'm very happy with my decision to stick with AA
because I get to hang with folks who have seen the dark side of life and have chosen to join the world of the living.
A lot of good people full of mirth and joy.
 Thankyou God for my life,

Sincerely Eric L

HOPE

My name is Hope I am an alcoholic. My sobriety date is 1-1-2011. I say that to remind myself that my sobriety has to come first. I started drinking at 21. I started coming around the rooms though when I was 17 with my then husband. I wasn't like him or so I thought.

Life continued down the path of destruction. When I took my first drink, I knew I found what I was looking for in that bottle of Jim Beam. He was my friend he never let me down. I drank and divorced first husband and married his best friend. Still didn't see a problem with my drinking. I continued to dry up for little bits of time until it came to work the steps and every time I came to the Fourth, I walked out again. I refused to do it.

In 2006 when I lost my children due to my actions, I turned to alcohol even more and divorced my second husband. Just didn't care anymore.

We moved states we changed everything. But where I went, I was there. It was bad.

I moved back to West Virginia and went back to my old stomping grounds with the same people I partied with before, and continued to do the same things and kept getting drunk for the next 5 years, it was that way.

I was with my ex-boyfriend then and we would always drink and party, it was our lives. On the day before the new year 2011. I sat down and cried. I couldn't get drunk anymore it wasn't fun. I hated who I had become. I wanted to die. I cried out "God help me!" and I remembered a few years before this that my friend who had known me the whole time in West Virginia, had given me his number and told me to call when I was ready to quit.

I looked for that number, I didn't think I would find it, but I did.

I called him and asked for help.

It was midnight by then. He came and got me and took me to a meeting. He just asked me on the way if I was done.

I said yes. He asked what I was and for the first time in my life I said

I am an alcoholic and I meant it. OMG really, I admitted I was an alcoholic. I felt so helpless and hopeless. That when we got to the meeting there was this lady that sat in the corner she walked up to me and she said, "I am your sponsor you will call me every day and you will go to three meetings a day." I agreed because I knew I couldn't and wouldn't do it alone. I needed her and if she told me to stand on my head in the corner, I would have. I needed you people and I knew I needed help. I jumped right into service and did what I needed to do. If my sponsor said pick this person up and do this I did it. It wasn't suggestions to me and I needed those hard people. Today I have a relationship with my children. They tell me they love me today. I am

here because I was willing to go to any lengths to stay sober and stay out of my own way. I am remarried for the 3rd time and my husband has never seen me take a drink. Sure, life still happens, however, I don't need a drink to get through it. A drink will not make anything any better for any reason. In recovery I have lost my mom and my grandmother's to cancer. I have fought and beat cancer, hearing loss, and didn't have to drink over it. Today I am a home owner. Me a homeowner never would have

thought it. I also have my own business. WOW. Sobriety has been amazing.

Nothing says things will be all perfect however we get through it the best we can. I call my sponsor I help others and go to meetings because that is what works for me, and I am forever grateful for it. Thanks for

letting me share my story. Hope H Michigan

Here are the 12 Steps as defined by Alcoholics Anonymous:

1. We admitted we were powerless over alcohol–that our lives had become unmanageable.
2. Came to believe that a Power greater than ourselves could restore us to sanity.
3. Made a decision to turn our will and our lives over to the care of God as we understood Him.
4. Made a searching and fearless moral inventory of ourselves.
5. Admitted to God, to ourselves and to another human being the exact nature of our wrongs.
6. Were entirely ready to have God remove all these defects of character
7. Humbly asked Him to remove our shortcomings
8. Made a list of persons we had harmed, and became willing to make amends to them all.
9. Made direct amends to such people wherever possible, except when to do so would injure them or others.
10. Continued to take personal inventory and when we were wrong promptly admitted it.
11. Sought through prayer and meditation to improve our conscious contact with God as we understood Him, praying only for knowledge of His will for us and the power to carry that out.
12. Having had a spiritual awakening as the result of these steps, we tried to carry this message to alcoholics and to practice these principles in all our affairs.

Here are the 12 traditions:

1. Our common welfare should come first; personal recovery depends upon AA unity.
2. For our group purpose there is but one ultimate authority–a loving God as He may express Himself in our group conscience. Our leaders are but trusted servants; they do not govern.
3. The only requirement for AA membership is a desire to stop drinking.
4. Each group should be autonomous except in matters affecting other groups or AA as a whole.
5. Each group has but one primary purpose–to carry its message to the alcoholic who still suffers.
6. An AA group ought never endorse, finance, or lend the AA name to any related facility or outside enterprise, lest problems of money, property and prestige divert us from our primary purpose.
7. Every AA group ought to be fully self-supporting, declining outside contributions.
8. Alcoholics Anonymous should remain forever nonprofessional, but our service centers may employ special workers.
9. AA, as such, ought never be organized; but we may create service boards or committees directly responsible to those they serve.
10. Alcoholics Anonymous has no opinion on outside issues; hence the AA name ought never be drawn into public controversy.
11. Our public relations policy is based on attraction rather than promotion; we need always maintain personal anonymity at the level of press, radio and films.
12. Anonymity is the spiritual foundation of all our traditions, ever reminding us to place principles before personalities.

ALCOHOLICS ANONYMOUS
Search the INTERNET for contact details
in your country.

Meetings are also available online.

aaonline.org

Al-Anon Alateen
For family and friends of problem drinkers.
al-anon.org

Lightning Source UK Ltd.
Milton Keynes UK
UKHW040302260219
338009UK00003B/106/P

9 780368 279102